P2P Investing 101

Why the Smart Money Invests in Peer to Pe

Table of Contents

Introduction

The purpose of this book is to compare the new asset class of peer to peer lending/p2p lending/marketplace lending (terms used interchangeably in the book) to other investments available on the market today. I've written it with the new investor to peer to peer lending in mind.

It's my view that p2p lending is a great investment with terrific potential over a long period of time. Peer lending is not just an adequate substitute, but a necessary replacement for one of the market's most conventional investment assets. A well-diversified investment portfolio requires investment in many asset classes. P2P lending is an asset class that needs to be part of the portfolio of the present and the future.

I hope if you agree, and especially if you disagree with this thesis or anything in this book that you will come to my blog at P2PLendingExpert.com and comment on it. The industry has been ever-changing since I started following it in 2013 and change keeps on coming. I can't wait to see what's next. You can subscribe for free to get tips and techniques for profitable investment right to your email each month.

Read on to see why peer to peer lending is a necessary choice in building a diversified and profitable portfolio for the long term.

Chapter 1: Common Investment Asset Classes

Anytime investments are the topic of discussion, the word you hear is Diversification.

Why?

Because Modern Portfolio Theory from back in 1952 dictates that we build a consistent and profitable portfolio with our investments by diversifying into different asset classes[1].

Just because we may have an interest in p2p lending or some other investment besides the typical investment options doesn't mean we should ignore these long established rules. The rules still apply today. To build your own long term profitable portfolio you need different assets and peer to peer lending should be among them. Let's check out the asset classes we have to choose from.

Stocks

Stocks, and by this I mean individual stock and stock mutual funds, are the bread and butter of a modern investment portfolio. Huge mutual fund companies like Vanguard and Fidelity got their enormous size of $4 trillion[2] and $2.1 trillion[3] in assets under management on the idea that Americans need to buy stocks to invest and save for retirement. Mutual fund companies make it easier to do so.

Stocks are an important investment class since ownership of stock means ownership of part of the company. You have an equity stake in that business. When you buy individual stock you need to choose wisely and when you buy a stock mutual fund you need to make sure

---

[1] http://www.investopedia.com/walkthrough/fund-guide/introduction/1/modern-portfolio-theory-mpt.aspx
[2] https://about.vanguard.com/who-we-are/fast-facts/
[3] https://www.fidelity.com/about-fidelity/overview

the fund's objectives like Aggressive Growth or Growth and Income match your own objectives like this Fidelity Fund whose fund objective is Large Growth (as shown here by Morningstar Fund Category, where Morningstar is an independent investment research service). Large growth here means growth from large company stocks.

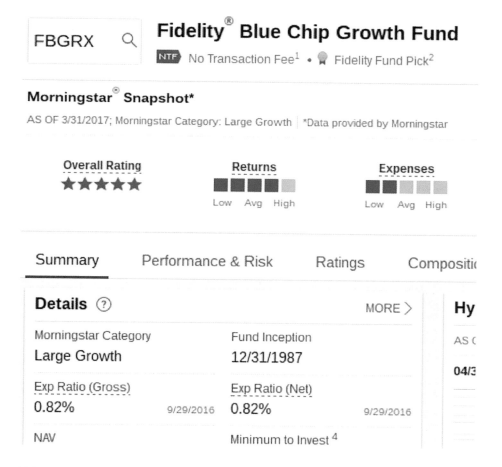

With any fund, the objective is important since your investment is diversified over many, many stocks. Here you buy a piece of the entire portfolio as opposed to a direct equity stake that you have in a company with the individual stock.

Drawback: Most investors have too much of their total investments in stocks and the stock market in mid-2017 is at exceptionally high (some would say speculative or risky) levels. If retirement is many years away, then keep investing. If your retirement is looming, you may want to consider other asset classes. We only have to go back a few years to the Great Recession to see how far markets can move against us and how long it takes for markets to recover.

Bonds

Unlike stock where you own a piece of the company, with a bond, you own an obligation (a debt) of the company. When you buy a government bond, the government is the debtor and you are the debt holder. The government is obligated to pay you based on the terms of the bond.

Like stock, here when I say bonds I mean both bonds and bond mutual funds.

This sounds complicated but a bond is no different than any other term loan like a mortgage. Your home mortgage is a fixed payment at a fixed rate over a 15 or 30 year period of time. If you have a variable rate mortgage, then your rate varies but your payment is fixed for a certain period of time like 1 year or 3 years.

Bonds are also known as fixed income investments as the income they generate through the fixed payment on the loan doesn't change. The only thing that changes in your returns as a bondholder are changes in interest rates and non-payment. Changes in interest rates only matter if you want to sell your bond before the end of the term, known as maturity.

Here's how a change in interest rates affects the price of a bond you may want to sell

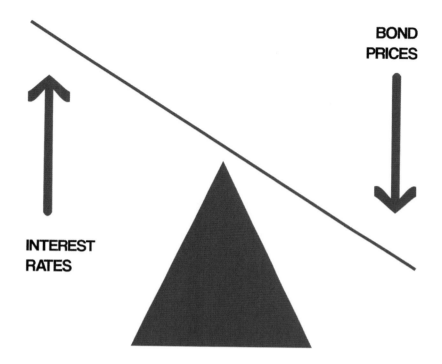

Rates and Prices Oppose Each Other

Since all bonds start at par value of 100 or 1000, you can see that the value of the bond changes and has an inverse (opposite) relationship to interest rates. The reason why is that a new investor who buys your bond expects to receive whatever the market interest rate is at the time they buy. So if the interest rate increases from 3% to 5%, then the bond price drops. The 3% coupon (or regular monthly or quarterly) payment on the bond doesn't change but now your bond buyer can get 5% elsewhere. Your bond buyer needs to get 5% from you if you sell, so your bond goes down in value so your coupon payment of the same dollars now equals 5% to the new buyer instead of 3%.

Types of Bonds

There are 2 types of bonds: Government and Corporate.

Government bonds are issued by the US Government (cities issue Municipal bonds) and guide everything from mortgage loan rates to inflation to how the US Treasury circulates money into the economy through the Federal Reserve.

Corporate bonds are bonds issued by a company usually to fund some specific needs and projects. Corporate bonds get a rating from an agency like Fitch, Moody's or S&P and the rating determines the interest rate the company pays on the bond.

Since a bond is a debt obligation, the company is obligated to pay you first before they pay their stockholders in the event of a corporate bankruptcy. Stockholders are usually paid AFTER bondholders. Yet, there is one prominent time when this did not happen: GM.

Instead of getting paid first, the Government forced GM bondholders to swap their bonds for equity in a new recapitalized GM with Federal ownership as part of their bailout. The government sold their stake at a profit and the bondholders, who chose to buy the bonds instead of the stock when they first invested, got stuck with equity they didn't want and have **never** been fully repaid.

When GM got its bailout by the Federal Government, the Feds screwed GM bondholders as explained in this Washington Post editorial[4]. Because GM did not liquidate the company upon its bankruptcy (and manipulated these laws due to the Great Recession), bondholders did not get paid. In fact, they got royally screwed[5]. Bondholders exchanged $70,000 in GM debt for a whopping $200 in stock. That is definitely screwed.

---

[4] http://www.washingtonpost.com/wp-dyn/content/article/2009/05/25/AR2009052502135.html
[5] http://www.darwinsmoney.com/gm-bonuses-bondholders/

There are tons of books on bonds as an investment. They are beyond the scope of this book. We do a deeper dive into bonds as an investment with some important comparisons in Chapter 3.

Drawback: The GM bailout and treatment of the bondholders is the first time, but probably not the last, that bondholders will get the short end of the stick. It outlines a much bigger problem that the risk/return ratio (where higher risk should equate to higher potential returns on an investment) is way out of whack in bonds. Bond rates are historically low, and many experts in 2017 say the rates are even artificially low and due for an increase.

Real Estate

Real estate is a common asset for an investment portfolio whether it is a personal residence or other real estate investments like land, buildings or 2nd homes held for investment purposes.

The biggest benefit for holding real estate is that it is an asset that is a protection against inflation. Increases in price levels overall almost always equate to an increase in real estate prices. Real estate also, usually, does not move in the same direction at the same time as the stock market. Real estate usually makes money if held for a long enough term, even if you bought a property at the top of the market before the Great Recession began.

The other biggest benefit most of us are more aware of about real estate as an investment is the use of leverage. Since you borrow and get mortgages to buy property, you get to take advantage of putting in a small amount of money to control a much higher valued asset. You get to participate in the profits during a rising market and losses and foreclosures like during the Great Recession.

One thing I have heard recently about real estate as an investment that I think is smart advice is to not count your own personal residence as an asset when building your diversified portfolio. Why?

Because you have to live someplace. This is a conservative viewpoint especially when the home is the average American's largest single asset, but I like this idea.

You have to decide for yourself when building your portfolio of how much value you put on your personal residence as an investment asset.

Drawback: Real estate is often illiquid. Even in 'hot' markets, it can take time to sell, settle and close a piece of real estate. The marketplace for real estate can be volatile due to the high leverage. Very good to excellent personal credit is required to get into a real estate investment as is a sizable down payment for investment properties, even when you factor in the leverage. 20% of $500,000 to buy a small building is still $100,000 that you have to come up with to make it happen.

I'm no real estate expert but there are many on Amazon or the retail bookstore of your choice to read up more on the various types of Real Estate investing available.

And while every one of these conventional asset classes has its drawbacks, they are the foundation of a strong investment portfolio and each should be considered on its own merits and as part of a cohesive investment strategy.

Alternative Assets

Almost everything that isn't considered a stock, bond (or mutual fund holding either or both) or real estate is considered an alternative asset. I will mention them for a moment here as a couple of these alternative assets are getting a chapter of their own for more analysis. Marketplace lending is in this category.

Without a doubt the most discussed alternative asset is Gold. Gold is THE safe haven asset. When it looks like the world is on fire, people turn to gold. When people think markets are too risky and over inflated they turn to gold. You get the idea.

Commodities are another alternative asset. They can be
- metals like gold and silver
- foodstuffs like wheat, corn, soybeans or coffee, or
- other goods like oil and gas

You can buy these assets or, the more common investment method, buy a contract that allows you to buy the asset with leverage. For instance, the price of Corn is 358 in this chart, that's cents or $3.58 per bushel. To buy a contract of Corn means you are buying 5000 bushels or ~$18,000 worth of Corn. Yet, you can control one Corn contract for $2025 at the Chicago Board of Trade (CBOT) so you get leverage here as well just like with Real Estate almost 9 to 1. Here's a price chart from Tradingcharts.com on Corn.

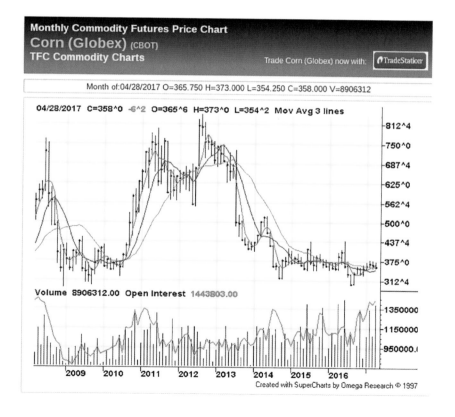

Monthly Commodity Futures Price Chart
Corn (Globex) (CBOT)
TFC Commodity Charts

Trade Corn (Globex) now with: TradeStation

Month of:04/28/2017 O=365.750 H=373.000 L=354.250 C=358.000 V=8906312

04/28/2017 C=358^0 -6^2 O=365^6 H=373^0 L=354^2 Mov Avg 3 lines

Volume 8906312.00 Open Interest 1443803.00

Created with SuperCharts by Omega Research © 1997

Foreign currencies are another alternative asset. Like commodities, you can buy a contract to hold British pounds (GBP) or Euros (EUR) or Swiss Francs (CHF). You can also buy the currency itself and hold a couple different ways including a foreign bank account or online payments service.

I take advantage of this myself and hold a nominal amount of Norwegian Kroner (NOK) at the time of this writing. In the case of this asset, it's an attempt to diversify outside the dollar but not into a direct asset (like real estate or stock) just into the currency itself.

One of the wealthy's secret alternative assets has a real estate component but is a true alternative: Timber. Timber is a great and consistent long term investment. It may surprise you to learn that you don't have to own the land to own its timber rights. Some places let you just buy the timber rights without having to own the land. Most do own the land they use for timber investment making it a productive land investment.

P2P Lending is one of these alternative assets as well. Our interest in these loans is not as the borrower but as the lender. We want to be lending the money and earning the interest just like a bank does on a loan. There are many many platforms available and most specialize in:

- Consumer Lending
- Real Estate Lending
- Student loans
- Small Business lending

Later chapters on the current market environment and how it compares to bonds will show you evidence that peer to peer/marketplace loans don't correlate with the stock market or the bond market making them a true alternative investment.

Summary

A well-diversified investment portfolio contains different types of assets. Conventional investment asset choices include stocks, bonds, mutual funds and real estate. Less conventional 'alternative' assets include Gold, silver, other commodities, foreign currencies, timber and p2p/marketplace loans. The best portfolios have a mix of conventional and alternative assets so no one market's performance can bring down the entire portfolio's value.

Chapter 2: Alternative Assets as Part of Your Portfolio

We just went over most of the asset classes we tend to invest in, so now we're going to look at alternative asset classes. Let's see where they fit into a standard portfolio in more detail. Other than peer to peer lending, there are two alternative assets that stand out.

Gold

Gold is a favored investment by many people for all kinds of reasons. Some like it cause they believe it's a finite asset. Others like that gold can't be easily reproduced like fiat government issued currencies. Some view Gold as a form of money like back in the Middle Ages or biblical times. Some see it as a risk-averse investment if Dollar or Euro-based assets get too expensive. Some cultures, especially in Asia in places like India and China, value gold as a way to hold assets outside their home currency and for use in celebrations like weddings.

Famous trader Jim Cramer recommends 10% of your portfolio in Gold[6]. Investing website Seeking Alpha compares different allocations of gold for a portfolio even up to 30%, not that they recommend this much invested in gold for most people[7].

The bottom line is that many people all over the world LOVE gold.

But how good of an investment is it?

If millions and millions of people love gold, is it a true alternative investment?

---

[6] http://www.cnbc.com/2016/03/03/cramer-best-insurance-policy-for-your-portfolio.html
[7] https://seekingalpha.com/article/1889651-30-percent-gold-in-a-diversified-portfolio

Low Correlation to Stock Market

The most common conventional asset for long term investment is Stocks. Seeing how Gold performs in relation to stocks would make sense in evaluating its alternative-ness. The Chicago Mercantile Exchange (known as the CME or the Merc) has done some research for us already[8]. Not coincidentally, the Merc is where gold contracts are traded....

The comparable assets are US Treasuries for bonds, the S&P 500 for stocks and Gold.

Figure 3: Low Correlations = Good Diversification

Correlation Table	1928 – 2015 Annual Data	1985 to 2015 Daily Futures Data
U.S. Treasuries & S&P 500®	0.00	-0.03
U.S. Treasuries & Gold	-0.02	-0.06
S&P 500® & Gold	-0.09	-0.01

Source: Federal Reserve Bank of St Louis, NYU Stern School of Business, Bloomberg Professional (TY1, SP1 and GC1) for raw data with calculations performed by CME Economic Research.

First, an explanation of correlation. Correlation is a scale between -1 and 0 and 0 and 1. A number close to 1 like 0.8 would mean a positive (number) correlation between the assets. Correlated assets are likely to behave similarly to each other during a specific event. For instance, if the market drops 5% in one day correlated assets would also likely drop. A number close to Zero means there is a low correlation. A negative number like -0.8 means the assets are INVERSELY correlated. This means that the assets move in opposite directions of each other. In our 5% drop in one day example, one asset may drop by 5% and the other would increase by 3%. That's negative correlation.

Back to the chart, over 2 extended periods of time, Gold shows virtually no correlation to either stocks or bonds since the correlations range from 0 down to -0.09, which means no correlation but no

---

[8] http://www.cmegroup.com/education/featured-reports/gold-useful-portfolio-diversifier.html

inverse correlation either. Gold does not move opposite of stocks or bonds or there would be larger negative numbers for inverse correlation.

Gold does its own thing making it a true alternative investment.

The Biggest Risk in Gold
Gold is a true alternative investment class. We see this by looking at correlation to other common investments. Many investment advisers and financial planners think you should have no more than 10% of your portfolio in gold, not just Jim Cramer who I quoted and linked to earlier. This is one of those common rules of thumb that investment people use.

There is one primary drawback to gold that you should be aware of: Gold certificates and e-Gold. Gold in the form of coins or bars is tough to store and transport so companies started creating certificates that are redeemable in gold. People buy these certificates instead of holding gold. The problem is many people believe (and I am among them) that there are more certificates redeemable in gold than there is gold to redeem them. If you buy gold, buy coins or bars and store them yourself.

Foreign Currencies
The US isn't the biggest or most populated country in the world. But the US Dollar is the biggest, most powerful currency in the world. That may change someday (and I think it will) but for now, the USD is still king.

The primary reason has to do with foreign trade. Let's say two countries want to do business with each other like Spain and Argentina. Argentina has great beef and Malbec wine and Spain wants some. What currency does this trade transact in for the countries? Euro since Spain is an EU country? No. Pesos since that is Argentina's currency? No. They MUST under the current trade system transact this deal in US Dollars. Spain has to swap for dollars and

Argentina has to swap for dollars. American banks earn a fee to do so like a toll road. Note that the American bank isn't involved in the deal any other way, yet our banking system earns fees to convert to USD and then back out to the other currencies. This system also means that every central bank all around the world needs to hold some dollars in their reserves.

By far, the largest trading market in the world with over 1 trillion daily is the foreign currency exchange or forex market.

So it makes sense that if we are thinking of building a portfolio that is diversified that we may want to include at least some other assets denominated in a different currency. After all, our stocks, bonds, mutual funds and US real estate are all denominated in dollars. What if the dollar loses value faster than other major currencies around the world?

Low-ish Negative Correlation
For our purposes of evaluating foreign currencies as an alternative asset, we are going to use the US Dollar Index (USDX). The USDX tracks the dollar's value against a basket of 6 other major currencies: Swiss Franc, Japanese Yen, Euro, Canadian Dollar, British Pound and the Swedish Krona.

Investopedia, one of my favorite investment sites, did some analysis of the USDX against the S&P 500. They also did the Dow Jones Industrial Average and the Nasdaq but we are using the S&P as our benchmark for stocks. They found a correlation of 0.38 for the S&P 500. This means that as the S&P 500 increases the USDX also increases but by less.

But we are looking for the opposite effect, not what the USD does but what the foreign currencies do. The USDX rises as the dollar increases against the basket of currencies. So the reality is that as stocks rise, it is likely that the basket of currencies drops in value in relation to the USD. The currencies are negatively correlated but not always[9].

It is important to note that this correlation is against these 6 currencies only. The currency you choose (a major like the Australian dollar or an exotic/emerging currency like the Chilean Peso) matters a lot. What also matters is if you are just holding currency, opening a bank account and you earn interest or are you holding an asset like stocks or land in that foreign currency.

What we want to see is holding a foreign currency is an alternative and not correlated asset to stocks and it is at least some of the time.

Summary

The two most common alternative assets on the market today are Gold and Foreign Currencies. Gold trades primarily in USD and foreign currencies can trade both against each other or against USD. We used correlation to see if these two assets had a positive correlation, negative correlation or no correlation. Gold is not correlated at all to the US stock market where Foreign currencies, depending on which one, can be not correlated or negatively (inversely) correlated. These are good features for inclusion of an asset in building a portfolio that can be profitable over a long period of time against many different sets of market conditions.

9

https://www.mcoscillator.com/learning_center/weekly_chart/the_real_relation
ship_between_dollar_and_stock_market/

Chapter 3 What are Government and Corporate Bonds?

Fixed income yields are terrible right now.

You know you need to build a portfolio of more than just stocks to manage risk properly. The best portfolios have different asset classes in them that don't correlate with each other, aiding us in proper risk management. We need both stocks and fixed income to build a long-term profitable portfolio.

With these horrible yields in fixed income, how do you accomplish this in today's market and make money?

Let's look at some of these fixed income options and see how they compare.

Long Term Government Bonds

It doesn't seem like that long ago when government bonds were considered the 'risk-free' investment. Portfolio calculations of risk took the risk premium based on the actual or potential returns over and above Treasuries. After all, the US Government was never going to default on a debt, right? Well, that used to be true. Confidence in our government to do anything is low at the moment and that lack of confidence extends to government bonds and how they might perform in the future.

The longest term US Government Bond, the 30 year, has a rate that is right around 2.5%[10]. This is low by all historical standards.

---

[10] https://www.treasury.gov/resource-center/data-chart-center/interest-rates/Pages/Historic-LongTerm-Rate-Data-Visualization.aspx

Today, inflation is near 1%. This means a real interest rate of 1.5% on bonds. Is that rate high enough to compensate you for the risk of holding onto a government bond for 30 years?

For most people, it isn't. Long term government bonds are an option, but a not great option when it comes to balancing the risk/reward ratio.

Summary
Type: Long Term Government Bond
Term: 10 to 30 years
Risk: Moderate (higher than people think it is). The greatest risk is not keeping up with inflation.
Quality of Investment: Returns not great for real risks involved and very long term required to hold.

Sovereign wealth funds, governments, and endowments need to keep buying Treasury bonds as it is one of the only markets large enough to absorb all the buying they have to do to put that money to work. Even at these paltry interest rates….

We are not a sovereign wealth fund. We have more choices.

Short Term Government Bonds (T-Bills)
T-Bills have much shorter terms ranging from one month to one year. The rate for one-month T-Bills is 0.254% and for one year is 0.642%[11]. With an annual inflation rate of 1%, we have a nominal real rate of return on the one-month T-Bills and are losing money to inflation if we hold T-Bills for one year.

One year T-Bills are obviously not a good investment.

The one month at 0.254% monthly over 12 months does give you a positive real rate of return on your money ((0.254%*12) or 3.048% - 1% inflation), but some of that return is eaten up with transaction

---

[11] https://www.treasurydirect.gov/instit/annceresult/annceresult.htm

costs since you have to buy new T-Bills each month meaning 12 transaction costs per year.

Summary
Type: T-Bills (Short Term Government Bonds)
Term: up to 1 year
Risk: Low
Quality of Investment: The shorter the term, the better and a good place to park cash for a short period of time. One year has a negative real interest rate.

T-Bills have their place especially for holding cash in a short term, temporary way while waiting to deploy funds into a more effective long term investment.

Now that we have looked at US government bonds, let's look at some more options.

Corporate Bonds

If you are on a quest for yield, the US Government as the bond issuer is not the place for you. We've seen that they don't do great on our risk/reward scale either.

Since large companies issue bonds too, we need to give corporate bonds a look.

Corporate bonds are underwritten by an investment bank and issued with a rating from one of the 3 big rating agencies: S&P, Moody's or Fitch. Corporate bonds should be a higher yield option for the fixed-income part of your portfolio. Yields on corporate bonds, like government bonds, have been in steady decline over the last few years too.

A quick glance at some corporate bonds from the NY Times shows some bonds by rating.

For instance, Verizon, who is BBB+ rated by S&P is yielding 5.24% on a 30 yr bond. Abbott Labs, who is BBB rated by S&P, is yielding 3.86% on a 10 yr bond. Johnson & Johnson, rated AAA by S&P is yielding just a hair over its coupon at 3.04% on a 10 yr bond.

FINRA TRACE Corporate Bond Data

03/17/2017

| INVESTMENT GRADE | HIGH YIELD | CONVERTIBLES |

Issuer name (symbol)	Coupon %	Maturity	Credit rating Moody's	S.&P.	Fitch	Price Last	Change	Yield %
Johnson & Johnson JNJ4340193	2.45%	Mar '12026	Aaa	AAA	AAA	95.418	+0.468	3.04%
Verizon Communications Inc VZ4466757	4.13%	Mar '12027	NR	BBB+	A-	100.856	+0.27	4.02%
Sumitomo Mitsui Finl Group Inc SMFG4381271	2.06%	Jul '12021	A1	A-	n.a.	96.905	−0.105	2.83%
Total Cap Cda Ltd TOT3954266	1.45%	Jan '12018	Aa3	A+	AA-	100.062	+0.303	1.37%
Bnp Paribas / Bnp Paribas Us Medium Term BNPQF3900102	2.38%	Sep '12017	A1	A	A+	100.334	+0.051	1.67%
Verizon Communications Inc VZ4466641	5.50%	Mar '12047	NR	BBB+	A-	103.955	+1.03	5.24%
Petroleos Mexicanos PEMX4342501	4.50%	Jan '12026	Baa3	BBB+	BBB+	96.306	+2.31	5.02%
Abbott Labs ABT4427939	3.75%	Nov '12026	Baa3	BBB	BBB	99.12	+0.194	3.86%
Altria Group Inc MO.HC	9.70%	Nov '12018	A3	A-	BBB+	112.542	+0.083	n.a.
Verizon Communications Inc VZ4466640	5.25%	Mar '12037	NR	BBB+	A-	102.51	+0.493	5.05%

To find a double-digit yield, we had to search for a D rated (by S&P) bond with a 2022 maturity for Chesapeake Energy (CUSIP: CHK4116807) to find a yield of exactly 10.00%. A D rating means they have already failed to pay on at least one of their other obligations and a default is likely[12]. A 10% rate is not exactly how you (or we) should be compensated for that kind of risk. And we have to hold this bond and hope they pay for 5 more years.

If you want to gamble you should go to Vegas, not gamble just to earn 10%.

This chart from the NY Times shows yields for investment-grade and high yield corp bonds

---

[12] https://info.creditriskmonitor.com/Help/SNPGlossary.asp

FINRA TRACE Corporate Bonds

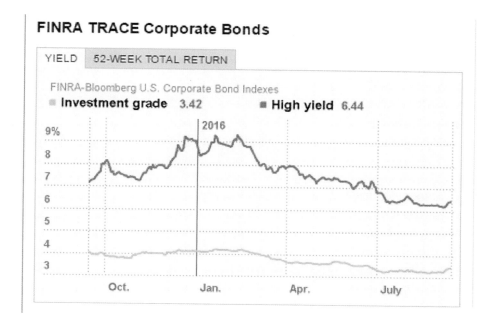

YIELD   52-WEEK TOTAL RETURN

FINRA-Bloomberg U.S. Corporate Bond Indexes
- **Investment grade**   3.42   ■ **High yield**   6.44

As you can see, rates are low at 3.42% for investment grade and 6.44% for high yield, which the market refers to as "junk" bonds. These rates are pretty slim for the risk we are taking. They do present some yield over and above US Gov't bonds though.

Remember we are in a historically low-interest rate environment. For all these bonds, but especially corporate bonds, if interest rates rise then the value of our bonds will fall.

Who knows how long these historically low-interest rate levels will last?

Summary
Type: Corporate Bonds
Term: Up to 30 years
Risk: Moderate on Short Term, High on Long Term and Junk
Quality of Investment: Investment grade bonds, especially in the short term, are probably solid. The longer the term and higher the yield the more uncertain due to rate environment and poor credits on the junk bonds.

This would be a good time to remind you of the corporate bondholder issues related to GM that I discussed in Chapter 1. It's important to remember that the real risks for bondholders do not price in items like government intervention resulting in a higher true risk for bond investors. How highly rated do you think GM was prior to their bankruptcy? 5 years prior? 10 years prior?

If government bonds and corporate bonds are either low yielding or too low yielding for the risk you are taking, then how do you allocate the fixed income requirement of your investment portfolio?

Peer to Peer/Marketplace Loans

To be a good fixed income investment, we need something that encompasses borrowing and steady repayment over time. We need to be able to select the type and average term of the loans we want.

And we need to get compensated for our risk.

Peer to Peer loans are a bet on a specific part(s) of the US economy. There are platforms that only do small business lending, or student loan refinancing or prime borrower (the best credits) unsecured consumer borrowing. US consumer lending is so large that if it was a country it would have the world's 6th largest GDP.

In this space, Lending Club gets the most looks and the most talk because they have been publicly traded for a while now. They are not the only platform out there.

Prosper, who is privately held, swims in the same pool that Lending Club does. Kabbage and Funding Circle are small business lenders. P2BInvestor does business receivables financing. Realty Mogul, Fundrise, and Patch of Land do real estate lending.

Investments on different platforms can help you get the fixed income duration you are seeking and spread the risk around too.

Whether the loan is secured by assets or not, nearly every platform has interest rates above 5-6% and often in the double digits.

Funding Circle says the average investor can expect a rate of 7.3% after fees and non-payments[13]. Kabbage's rates are generally in the low teens when fees and rate are combined.

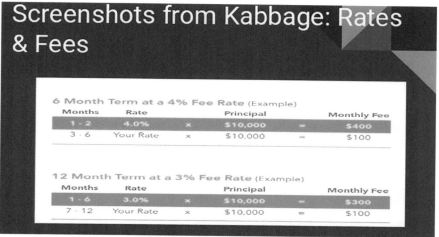

Lending Club's lowest rates are 5.32%-8.59% for A grade[14].

Just a small initial glance at p2p lending and the rates are much higher. On these platforms, we get paid for our risk.

So how do we choose which platforms and how do we invest wisely?

Chapters 6 and 7 cover all the primary investment options in p2p lending that are open to all investors.

So let's sum up peer loans compared to bonds

[13] https://www.fundingcircle.com/investors/rates-and-fees
[14] https://www.lendingclub.com/public/rates-and-fees.action

Summary

Type: Peer to Peer Loans

Term: 18 months to 5 years (usually)

Risk: Low on the Excellent Grade (A grades), Higher as you go to lesser credit grades

Quality of Investment: More flexibility and versatility for portfolio building based on risk, duration, rate. Some diversification as money spreads over many borrowers. Go get higher rates and the defaults that come with it or get lower, slower steadier rates or mix and match. Proper compensation for risk. The risk/reward works here. Does not correlate with other financial markets.

We will dive much deeper into this analysis in general and with the specific platforms in Chapter 6 & 7.

The only real downside to this market is that it has not experienced an economic downturn and we have no idea how these credits will react to that. The other fixed income options won't do so well with a drastic turn of economic events either. Corporate bonds, in particular, will do terribly when the next recession hits. Government bonds would get more attention and buying interest but bid up bond prices mean even lower rates and negative real rates for certain.

The only place in fixed income where we get paid for the risk we take is in peer to peer/marketplace loans. You need to take the portfolio building ideas of having stocks, bonds, cash, real estate and other assets and take the bond part out of this equation and substitute p2p lending for its fixed income potential instead.

Bonds do NOT pay us properly for our risk. Marketplace loans do and WE get to select the risks we want to take.

Chapter 4: Where P2P Lending Fits In The Investment Picture

We've looked at conventional assets and some of the most popular alternative assets. A deeper look into bonds shows areas of concern and risk where you may not get compensated for the real risks you take. The GM example shows some of the risks not factored into the pricing of corporate bonds. I suggested using p2p lending as a substitute for bonds. But why? And How?

Where does p2p lending fit into this picture?

The New Fixed Income Option

Marketplace Lending/Peer to Peer Lending is a newer arrival as an asset class. It has some important fixed income characteristics, especially in this low-interest rate environment that we have been in for quite a few years now.

Peer to Peer Lending intimidates people or they are unsure of it but it's only a different fixed income investment.

The most available fixed income investment option for building a portfolio is a bond. There are different types but the most popular are Government Bonds and Corporate Bonds, which is why they got Chapter 3 for a more detailed discussion.

Now we are going to look deeper at why P2P Lending is a good investment to add to your portfolio.

P2P Lending Portfolios are Quality Assets in Uncertain Times

Marketplace Lending is a desirable asset class to invest in for a couple of reasons including:
- the yields

- low risk
- lower volatility and
- lack of correlation with the stock market

Lending Robot[15](who is now part of NSR Invest), an automated investment service and robo-advisor for the industry, published a white paper in 2015 on volatility and correlation that still applies today. On page 6, they show a volatility study they did with results below.

Peer Lending vs Initial Portfolio

Asset	Annual Return	Volatility	Return-to-risk ratio
Initial Portfolio	0.069988096	0.403880638	0.17328906
Marketplace Lending	0.051782921	0.027057340	1.91382153

Their initial portfolio is a selection of various stock and bond mutual funds covering small-cap, mid-cap, growth & income, international and aggressive growth stocks as well as bonds. The returns are 5.1% per year for the peer loans versus 6.9% per year for the stock and bond funds, yet, the volatility is way, way less at 0.02 vs. 0.40.

Incorporating Marketplace Lending into a portfolio that has stocks and bonds in it appears to keep returns steady yet bring overall volatility way down. This could become an important factor in the increasing volatility and rate environment most believe will come in the next few years.

Another interesting part of the study is how P2P Lending assets don't correlate with the markets. Page 8 of the paper shows an analysis versus all the stock and bond funds used to create the initial portfolio for the study.

15

https://d2qh2u5m1l6y4n.cloudfront.net/media/other/howmuchtoinvest. pdf How Much Should You Invest in Marketplace Lending by Lending Robot

Assets Correlation

	VTI	VPACX	VEURX	VBR	VNQ	AGG	TIP	VWEHX	Mktpl Lending
VTI	1.00	0.85	0.88	0.96	0.82	0.08	0.09	0.75	0.19
VPACX	0.85	1.00	0.88	0.80	0.69	0.14	0.14	0.67	0.13
VEURX	0.88	0.88	1.00	0.82	0.71	0.14	0.15	0.70	0.14
VBR	0.96	0.80	0.82	1.00	0.86	0.07	0.07	0.72	0.13
VNQ	0.82	0.69	0.71	0.86	1.00	0.26	0.28	0.69	0.18
AGG	0.08	0.14	0.14	0.07	0.26	1.00	0.76	0.32	−0.13
TIP	0.09	0.14	0.15	0.07	0.28	0.76	1.00	0.33	−0.02
VWEHX	0.75	0.67	0.70	0.72	0.69	0.32	0.33	1.00	0.01
Mktpl Lending	0.19	0.14	0.14	0.13	0.18	−0.13	−0.02	0.01	1.00

Remember from Chapter 2 that correlations go between -1 and 1 with closer to 1 meaning more closely correlated. Negative (red) numbers mean they are inversely correlated like how bond rates and bond prices move in opposite directions from each other.

The highest correlation of 0.19 is not highly correlated between Peer Lending and a stock market mutual fund and interestingly, the 2 funds showing a negative correlation are both bond funds (an Aggressive Bond Fund and a TIP bond fund).

Marketplace lending platforms have many different options for types of investment like the mutual fund investment objective. There are more options based on the type of borrower with super prime, prime, near prime and subprime borrowers. The flexibility and number of platforms available mean more ability to control the credit risk you want to take in your portfolio. For instance, there are platforms that only work with super prime, high-income borrowers if reducing credit risk is a major concern.

Consumer peer lending platform Prosper Marketplace reports that their average FICO credit score is 701[16], just a hair higher than the

---

[16] https://www.prosper.com/invest

industry average of 695 and in the Prime category of the borrower. Another consumer platform Avant [17](not one of our big 7) goes lower with an average FICO between 600 and 700 putting it in the "near prime' and part of the subprime categories. Platform choice means you decide which credits you are comfortable buying.

Mutual fund data company Lipper[18] reported the week after the election ending 11/16 showed net outflows on bond funds of $5.9 billion and $0.9 billion for All bond funds and global and international bond funds, respectively. The investment manager pros are already cutting their exposure to bonds.

If you are like most people, then you don't know how to analyze small business credit, individual personal credit or analyze financial statements. Maybe you do know how and you just don't want to go through all that. So how do you select which loans to buy for your portfolio? It can be daunting.

One option is….

A Managed Fund

There are some private investment funds who only invest in peer loans from the various online lending platforms.

It's like a mutual fund but not of stocks or bonds, but of peer to peer loans. Unlike a mutual fund, it's a private investment fund and not public. Think of it like the sector specific ETFs out there like being able to buy the Basic Materials stocks from the S&P 500 if that's a sector you like. Again, unlike an ETF, it's *private,* not public.

---

[17] http://support.avant.com/article/14-avant-credit-quality
[18]
http://www.lipperusfundflows.com/#create:home:Home:/php/signup_trial.php

Like with stock mutual funds or ETFs where you buy diversification with smaller dollars, a managed fund is providing fixed income from many peer lending sources, not just a couple of platforms like if you had to pick them out yourself.

Prime Meridian and Direct Lending Investments work with accredited investors while Ranger and NSR Invest work with unaccredited retail investors. There are some other funds out there but these are among the best in class in the industry. As with all investments, do your research.

It's possible to diversify across different sets of borrowers, different loan purposes, different loan amounts and different loan terms, all with one investment in one place, a managed fund. Do your homework and due diligence if you pick one of these funds for investment.

What Are The Risks?
There are 3 major risks in marketplace lending.

No historical full economic cycle data: The oldest p2p lending platforms in the US were not operating at large volumes when the Great Recession took place. We as an industry have no data on a full economic cycle including boom and bust periods. We have no idea how these loans will react to a recession or other economic downturn. As discussed in Chapter 3, bonds would do poorly during that time except for some Government bonds that are seen as safe in tumultuous times. Will peer loans do worse than government bonds? Corporate bonds? We can guess but we don't know.

Liquidity: When we look at the platforms in more detail in Chapters 6 & 7, there are widely varying degrees of liquidity available. For instance, Lending Club & Prosper let you access your cash balance anytime, but you cannot liquidate your positions in active loans and there is no active secondary market. Once you invest in a piece of a loan, you are stuck with it. Some platforms have less liquidity than

Prosper so be sure you understand how you can get your funds and what investment time frames each platform is using. Are they short term loans with more access to liquidity or are they long term projects? Make sure you know when you invest.

Platform-specific Risk: Each platform has its own specific risks. This can include market, management, technology, operational effectiveness, and how they can raise money. For instance, be sure that the management team at a real estate lending platform has years of prior real estate lending and/or investing experience in properties in the more conventional markets before bringing it online. A market risk can mean that there's a real estate bubble burst (like we saw in 2009) and a platform is stuck with uncompleted projects and having to foreclose. It is platform specific risks like these that are why you must do your own due diligence and research on a platform before you decide to invest.

Do what you can to mitigate these risks, especially the last two since you can control which platform you invest in based on their liquidity standards and what you think of their management and operations.

Summary

As investors, you understand that fixed income is an asset class you need to have in your portfolio, somehow. It moves in unrelated ways to the stock market, which is important. But profitable, good yielding risk-appropriate options for fixed income investments are few.

Except for Marketplace Lending

If you want to diversify part of your portfolio into this one profitable area of fixed income, then a managed fund is one way to do so. You can add this emerging asset class to your portfolio without all the hassle of picking loans and platforms yourself. The professionals handle it for you.

You can also choose the option for greater control than a managed fund by investing on any one, or all, of the 7 platforms we examine in more detail later in the book. Personally managed or professionally managed, p2p lending should be your primary fixed income investment over bonds. There are risks although unlike most bonds we get paid for the risks we take.

Generate income from your fixed income portion of your portfolio where you are paid for your risk, can earn real returns that outpace inflation and take a slice out of one of the biggest markets in the country.

Chapter 5: P2P Lending In 2017

As the new fixed income option, let's look at peer to peer lending and its current outlook.

P2P Lending In a Good Position

The result of the 2016 Presidential election was a surprise to many people. Even the markets themselves had no idea how to react with futures down by more than 5% the night after the election, at first. Recovery from the drop was near immediate and the market has gained since then with the S&P 500 currently at 2441 . This theme of increased volatility will likely continue and p2p lending is in a position to benefit from the current market conditions and a new Presidential administration.

Economic Outlook

The Wall Street Journal is reporting that real GDP should grow for 2017 and 2018 to the 2.25% range with inflation and bond yields on the increase as well, as seen in this chart.

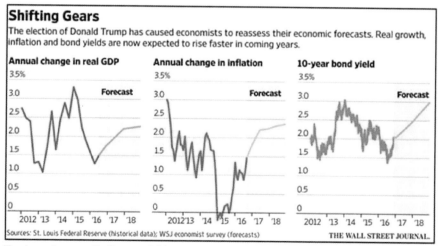

Shifting Gears

The election of Donald Trump has caused economists to reassess their economic forecasts. Real growth, inflation and bond yields are now expected to rise faster in coming years.

Sources: St. Louis Federal Reserve (historical data); WSJ economist survey (forecasts)

THE WALL STREET JOURNAL.

Forbes is predicting a 2% growth for 2016 and a slight growth rate of just over 3% for 2017[19]. In their notes from their late September and

October meetings, the Fed's FOMC (Federal Open Market Committee who sets national interest rate policy) forecasts 2% growth in 2017 and 2018. [20]

Summary: Many forecasters are saying that there will be nominal growth with perhaps slower growth than the last couple years for 2017 and 2018.

Market Reaction

In the meantime, investors look bullish on the US markets based on this Financial Times (FT) piece on equity flows[21]. The flows into stocks and stock funds are at near record levels. The FT piece goes on to say that these inflows are matching outflows from emerging market bond funds in markets like Mexico.

The market reaction is not limited to stock markets, inflation, and economic growth. There have been big movements in the currency markets as well. Here's how the dollar has done against other important currencies.

The WSJ reports the biggest gain in the USD against a basket of 16 currencies since May 2016 in the week immediately following the election[22]. The rally is 2.4% so far with more records set a week later on the US Dollar Index per FT[23]. Business Insider reported that the Mexican peso, an important currency due to the amount of trade we do with Mexico, was down to a new low right after the election of just over 20 MXN per USD[24]. The Chinese Yuan is down to almost 7 per 1

[19] http://www.forbes.com/sites/billconerly/2016/09/16/u-s-economic-forecast-2017-2018-mild-rebound/#4237ae5123b6
[20] https://www.thebalance.com/fomc-meetings-schedule-and-statement-summaries-3305975
[21] https://www.ft.com/content/783965aa-ad17-11e6-9cb3-bb8207902122
[22] http://www.wsj.com/articles/u-s-dollar-rally-finds-new-life-under-trump-1479067257
[23] on.ft.com/2fb38YT

USD. CNN is reporting a record high of the USD against other currencies as well[25].

Summary: The USD has increased against almost every major currency since the election. This is something that could continue or new trade policies could affect the USD against other currencies in an unknown way in the new administration. The stock market is reacting positively so far.

Remember back in Chapter 2, we examined currencies as an alternative asset due to their lack of correlation with the stock market.

Increased Volatility

Surprises like this election result usually mean uncertainty and uncertainty means volatility. CNBC reports an increase in volatility in the market already and expects this to continue[26]. The WSJ agrees that volatility should 'remain high' with quotes from economists and banks such as PNC and DeutscheBank's Asset Management Group[27]. The immediate reaction of a drop in all market futures before the open right after election day to the immediate recovery is a potential sign of the volatility to come based on the uncertainty of what a Trump administration might do.

The Dow hit a market high of just under 21,000 with an increase in volatility. The VIX, a measure of volatility and traded on its own on the CBOE, spiked from around 12 before election day up to 21.51 before dropping back to around 11.5 where it is today[28]. Morgan Stanley

---

[24] http://markets.businessinsider.com/currencies/news/Mexicos-markets-have-been-getting-rocked-since-Trump-won-USD-MXN-1001522071
[25] http://money.cnn.com/data/currencies/
[26] http://www.cnbc.com/2016/11/09/trumps-presidency-creates-market-volatility.html
[27] http://blogs.wsj.com/economics/2016/11/09/economists-react-to-donald-trumps-win-volatility-should-remain-high/)
[28]

https://finance.yahoo.com/chart/%5EVIX#eyJtdWx0aUNvbG9yTGluZ

agrees with the volatility and potential increases in rates and inflation. They maintain the position that the Fed will raise rates in December (2016 which they did)[29]. Unlike the other projections here, they see a potential buying opportunity based on sectors that may be oversold, as well as the potential for corporate profits, decreased regulation and tax policy under the new administration (so far we've seen some decreased regulations).

Two fund managers who asked not to be named, one at a large fund and one at a smaller fund, commented on the volatility as well. One told me that 'there is a bit of price volatility associated with markets and treasury rates that are having a minor effect in the [p2p lending] industry like any other short-dated, high yield fixed income investment, but which is being offset by positive news associated with some of the big platforms securing capital.' The other said that 'volatility is in a good place now and we are looking to deploy more funds into certain specialty marketplace platforms.'

Summary: The general consensus from bond market activity and the strategists is that rates will increase as well as inflation in an environment that will be more volatile than where we have been the last couple years. The new administration's tax and regulatory policies could benefit markets and investments when implemented.

If rates and inflation both increase, then where in fixed income are the buying opportunities?

Sl6ZmFsc2UsImJvbGxpbmdlclVwcGVyQ29sb3liOiljZTIwMDgxliwiYm
9sbGluZ2VyTG93ZXJDb2xvcil6IiM5NTUyZmYiLCJtZmlMaW5lQ29sb
3liOiljNDVIM2ZmliwibWFjZERpdmVyZ2VuY2VDb2xvcil6liNmZjdiMTli
LCJtYWNkTWFjZENvbG9yIjoilzc4N2Q4MilsIm1hY2RTaWduYWxDb2
xvcil6liMwMDAwMDAiLCJyc2lMaW5lQ29sb3liOiljZmZiNzAwliwic3Rv
Y2hLTGluZUNvbG9yIil2ZmYjcwMClsInN0b2NoRExpbmVDb2xvcil6
liM0NWUzZmYiLCJyYW5nZSI6IjF5In0%3D
[29] http://www.morganstanley.com/articles/trump-win-may-be-bond-buying-opportunity

Fixed Income Likely to Move to Credit Risk from Interest Rate Risk

A selloff in global bond markets means that US interest rates are at its highest level in a year[30]. The benchmark 10 year Treasury is up 50 basis points just since election day. The opinion in this same CNBC article shared by rate strategists at B of A Merrill Lynch, Nomura Securities and Brown Brothers Harriman is that an increase in rates is highly likely and will lead to an increase in inflation as well.

Summary: With this interest rate rise baked in, the fixed income markets are likely to move to an evaluation of credit risk instead of rate risk. Fixed Income options dealing with prime borrowers with high FICO credit scores, good incomes and good Debt to Income ratios are likely to take precedence in consumer and small business loan markets. Prime borrower loans will be in high demand in this changing market environment. Many marketplace lending platforms fit this description of borrower type leading to a reduction in credit risk.

Eventually the money going out of emerging bond funds into the US stock market like FT reports or flowing out bond funds altogether like Lipper reports will want to diversify in some way. Marketplace lending is a great option that won't correlate with your existing investments when you're ready to make the move. P2P Lending assets are quality assets for uncertain, volatile times.

The smart money is telling us that bonds are not the answer to the question of where are the fixed income buying opportunities.

More Options for Retail Investors

The amendment to old SEC Regulation A, known as Reg A+, means there are more marketplace lending options for non-accredited retail investors than ever before. This topic is so important to our (I'm not

---

[30] http://www.cnbc.com/2016/11/14/donald-trump-blew-up-the-bond-market-and-changed-everyones-view-of-interest-rates.html

accredited either) ability to invest that I cover it in depth in the next chapter so only a couple brief notes here.

While the impact of Reg A+ is meant to help make all crowdfunding easier, peer lending platforms are finding special uses for it to access retail dollars. That access means more people can invest in more peer lending opportunities than before the amendment. Prior to Reg A+, we only had options in the Consumer lending space and now that's no longer true.

Summary

A new administration brings some uncertainty into the investments world. Even with that uncertainty, p2p lending looks able to benefit from the changes we might see.

We have a positive economic outlook for the next couple years based on many projections of GDP growth of 2-3%. Markets have reacted positively with the Dow and S&P reaching new highs and the USD has gained in value against other major currencies. Volatility is on the increase and peer lending as part of a portfolio maintains steady returns and decreases volatility. Interest rates have risen since December creating a shift to credit risk in the fixed income markets. With more marketplace platforms to choose from, we can control how much credit risk we decide to take. Each of these factors benefits p2p lending as an investment option as part of profitable low-risk portfolio building.

Chapter 6: Reg A+ Means More Investment Options

Retail 'little guy' investors like us have the JOBS Act ,[31] passed in 2012, to thank for the amendment to Regulation A known as Reg A+. The nickname for Reg A+ is the mini-IPO (initial public offering) as most people in finance see it as a miniature version of access to public markets. In this chapter, we are going to look at Reg A+ and the 5 p2p lending platforms that are using it.

Reg A+ allows for access to public markets in a way that a standard IPO allows without the heavy costs, fees and compliance that a full IPO requires, thus the mini part.

Many companies are using Reg A+ to crowdfund for equity investment. While that is a great use for it, we are talking about marketplace lending so let's see how platforms are using Reg A+ in the peer to peer lending world.

First, a little more about what Reg A+ is and does and why it is important for us.

Two Investment Tiers

In 2015, the SEC released the final rules on how to use Reg A+ by offering 2 tiers of investment offerings[32]. Tier 1 allows companies to raise as much as $20 million in a 12 month period and Tier 2 allows up to $50 million in a 12 month period. The larger Tier 2 offering requires some added compliance like audited financial statements, annual reports, and a limit on the number of securities a retail/unaccredited investor can buy. That limit is no more than 10% of your annual income or net worth[33]. This is a self reporting requirement

---

[31] https://www.sec.gov/spotlight/jobs-act.shtml General announcement of JOBS Act

[32] https://www.sec.gov/news/pressrelease/2015-49.html Final Rules released

[33] https://www.sec.gov/news/pressrelease/2015-49.html See Additional Tier

but keep this in mind and a platform may ask you about your net worth if they have a Tier 2 offering.

For reasons that include compliance costs and amount of capital they can raise, most platforms opt for the Tier 2 offering. Crowdfund Insider has some excellent analysis on the difference between the tiers[34]. Their analysis is a great resource for those that want to learn more details about the topic.

Reg A+ Finds a Home in Real Estate

Reg A+ has sparked lots of creativity from companies to figure out how to best use it for raising funds. One of the most interesting developments in marketplace lending is that real estate platforms are the first to jump in and take advantage.

The one real estate investment that has been available to the public for many years is the REIT. REIT stands for Real Estate Investment Trust and at its core is a mutual fund like investment for real estate. When you buy shares of a REIT, you are buying a piece of every real estate investment they have in the trust. Just like how a stock mutual fund means you own a small piece of every stock in the portfolio, a REIT works exactly the same way except with Real Estate. Many REITs are publicly traded on the NYSE.

Until the implementation of Reg A+, the REIT was the only way you could invest in a property other than private partnerships or you buying a property for investment in your own community. Both options hold greater potential risk and return due to more funds invested into only 1 property.

If you are an accredited investor, then you have more choices. For unaccredited investors, there are 4 real estate platforms taking advantage of Reg A+.

Requirements
[34] https://www.crowdfundinsider.com/2016/09/90421-regulation-offering-hype-reality/

What follows is lots of information on different platforms so I have a handy table at the end of the chapter to help compare these platforms to each other. Here are the platforms one by one.

RealtyMogul

RealtyMogul offers their unique product using Reg A+ called the MogulREIT[35]. RealtyMogul offers both debt and equity investments and if you buy into the MogulREIT you will have exposure to both. Equity is often set up as your ownership in a LLC (a common tactic) that owns the property. Debt means you are the mortgage holder on the property. As a REIT, the MogulREIT must distribute at least 90% of its profits to its shareholders[36]. These rules apply whether it is a NYSE listed REIT or a private one like this one.

The MogulREIT I is sold out now and MogulREIT II is now open. MogulREIT II opened in August 2017 and invests in apartment buildings. The goal of this fund is to raise $50 million for investment in apartments.[37] Here is the SEC filing for the REIT.[38]

Minimum investment: $1000
Rates: Variable as there is debt and equity but they seek a 10%+ IRR (Internal Rate of Return)
Term: This is a long term investment
Liquidity: Redemptions allowed Quarterly & Dividends paid Quarterly
IRA accepted?: Yes, if your custodian is set up with electronic signatures for document execution and for real estate investment. If you want to invest with your IRA, then ask your custodian first. You

---

[35] https://www.realtymogul.com/resource-center/articles/realtymogulcom-launches-its-first-crowdfunded-real-estate-investment-trust Announcement of MogulREIT

[36] https://www.sec.gov/fast-answers/answersreitshtm.html

[37] https://www.crowdfundinsider.com/2017/07/118769-realtymogul-preps-mogulreit-ii-mogulreit-raised-15-5-million/

[38] http://pdf.secdatabase.com/1221/0001558370-17-006888.pdf from SECDatabase.com

may need to set up a self-directed IRA if your current custodian does not allow this type of investment.

Types of Properties: All commercial all across the country from multi-family, to office, industrial, hotel, or self storage. MogulREIT II is primarily apartment buildings.

Safety: The properties are your collateral

More Info: RealtyMogul.com and they have an excellent FAQ page, click on Invest in MogulREIT.

Here is the screenshot of the MogulREIT I as the MogulREIT II screenshots aren't available at the time of this writing.

Fundrise

Fundrise is another online lending platform using Reg A+. Like RealtyMogul they are using the REIT method of offering their investment to non-accredited investors. Fundrise is the creator of the e-REIT [39]. The e-REITs are a blend of debt and equity here as well.

When you check out the Fundrise e-REIT options on their site, you are going to see something familiar to you. If you have ever bought mutual funds then you know that each one has an investment objective that can be general like Global Growth or specific like Growth & Income, which means they can only invest in stocks that pay a dividend to cover the income part of the objective. Fundrise lists their REITs by investment objective (although the Growth e-REIT and the Income e-REIT are sold out and oversubscribed at the time of this writing) and also by geography. They have a West Coast REIT, an East Coast REIT and a Heartland REIT, just to name a few.

This is what the page and description of the East Coast E-REIT look like at Fundrise

These investment objectives make for a user friendly experience in evaluating their e-REITs as an investment.

---

[39] https://fundrise.com/education/faq What is a e-REIT?

As with all these platforms using Reg A+, they are required to give you a copy of their Offering Circular which is the prospectus for the trust. ALWAYS click that link and get your own copy of this document if you are considering investment.

Minimum investment: $1000
Rates: Variable as they have debt and equity. Seek 10%+ IRR
Term: This is a long term investment. See next one on Liquidity
Liquidity: Dividends paid out Quarterly. Redemptions allowed Quarterly but MAY be on a limited basis
IRA Accepted?: Yes, they have a custodial relationship with Millennium Trust for a self directed IRA if your custodian does not allow it.
Types of Property: All commercial real estate types. Lots of multi-family
Safety: The properties are your collateral
More Info: Fundrise.com and their FAQ page, as well as their E-REIT Portfolio Builder in the Learn section

GroundFloor

Unlike Fundrise and RealtyMogul, Groundfloor takes a different approach.

Do you ever watch any of the never-ending supply of fix and flip shows on HGTV and wonder where the rehabbers get the money to fund these projects? They certainly don't fund them only from their own money.

Until recently, they only used private money called Hard Money for short terms at very high interest rates. This is why you see the rush on those shows to finish getting the floors in so they can stage the home and put it on the market. Each month on the market means less profit for them when they have to make one more high interest payment.

Groundfloor was the first peer lending platform to use Reg A+[40].

Groundfloor brings online lending to the rehab/renovation market. When you invest on Groundfloor, it's debt only (no equity), backed by the property and only for a short term as that's the way the rehabbers want it. Thanks to short term rehab related loans, this is a different approach than the other platforms we've discussed so far. Along with the shortest term on each loan, they also have the lowest minimum per loan of $10. Yes, only $10.

Also, unlike the other platforms where you buy a piece of many projects, on Groundfloor you get to see all the projects available and lend as much or as little on each one as you like. This means much more control in loan selection.

Is it good to you that you have more control? Some want to invest more passively and others more actively.

Minimum Investment: $10
Rates: 10%+
Term: Very short term, maximum 12 mo loans
Liquidity: Funds are liquid at any time
IRA Accepted?: Yes, they work with IRA Services Trust as custodian if you don't have a custodian that allows this and you need a self directed IRA
Types of Property: Residential properties needing repairs
Safety: The property is your collateral
More Info: Their Learn page on their website groundfloor.us

AHP

Last real estate platform, but certainly not least, is AHP. AHP stands for American Homeowner Preservation. Like Groundfloor, they have a unique model. You are lending money to AHP so they can buy a pool of available loans only slightly different from the debt portion of the Fundrise and RealtyMogul options. There's no equity option with AHP.

---

[40] https://www.crowdfundinsider.com/2015/09/73636-groundfloor-claims-first-sec-approved-1-a-regulation-a-filing/

Check out this model. I'd never heard of anything like it that wasn't offered by a hedge fund. AHP goes in and buys a pool of defaulted mortgages at a discount. They use your money to buy the pool. AHP does not make any money until they pay you 12% interest. That amount is fixed so the platform is keeping all the upside over and above 12%. AHP now holds the mortgage for a lower amount against the property. The property is probably in mediocre or not well maintained condition.

Then, the real difference comes in.

AHP goes to the defaulted homeowner and sees if they are able to pay a reduced monthly payment to stay in the house. If they can, then they stay and convert the non-paying mortgage into a paying mortgage making it instantly more valuable. If they can't pay then they get time to move out and the property is sold, usually at a profit since the amount of the mortgage has been reduced.

Let's look at this with some numbers. That may make it easier to understand.

A $100,000 home with a $90,000 mortgage and payment of $750 is foreclosed upon. AHP buys the $90,000 mortgage for $55,000. The mortgage is non-performing so it sells at a steep discount. The home hasn't been well maintained so it's not worth $100,000 or $90,000. AHP calls the homeowner and tells them that we are going to write the mortgage down from $90,000 to $70,000 and bring the payment from $750 down to $565 per month. Can they afford that? Maybe they can if their reason for non-payment was job loss and now they have a new job. Homeowner says yes they can afford it and stay in the home. How did everyone do?

- **Homeowner**: Big win. Their mortgage and payment is down and they can stay in the house
- **AHP**: Big win. They converted their purchased mortgage from non-paying to paying. They are getting $565 per month AND

they have $15,000 equity in the note ($70,000-$55,000). AHP has lots of upside even after paying you your 12%.

- **You**: Big win. You earned 12%.

One thing is for sure. If you decide to invest with AHP, your money will be doing something different with them than with any other investment out there on the market today.

Minimum Investment: $100
Rates: 12% fixed (less if losses accumulate as rate is not guaranteed)
Term: 5 years
Liquidity: Funds are liquid at any time
IRA Accepted?: Yes, they work with IRA Services Trust as custodian if you don't have a custodian that allows this and you need a self directed IRA
Types of Property: Residential properties often with subprime mortgages
Safety: The property is your collateral
More Info: Their How It Works page at ahpfund.com

The 4 real estate platforms that use Reg A+: Fundrise, RealtyMogul, Groundfloor and AHP all have unique offerings to investors and all use Reg A+ in their own way. The creative uses of these new rules allow all four of these platforms to attract retail investor dollars onto their platforms.

One Small Business Platform

As I said at the top of this chapter, there are 5 online lending platforms using Reg A+. Four of them are in real estate and the 5th is in small business and they have a pretty cool angle to their business. The peer to peer small business lender is Streetshares.

Streetshares

Streetshares is a small business lender with an interesting twist. That twist is they focus on small businesses owned by veterans and their family members. Their use of Reg A+ is unique as well. They created a product they call the Veteran Business Bond. It's a one year term and pays a fixed 5%. Your money invests across all the Streetshares loans available at that time.

The minimum investment is only $25 and the maximum is $50,000. Your money is locked up for a year and at the end of that year you can choose to roll it over into another 12 month Veteran Business Bond or liquidate.

The great thing about this platform is its ethos. It not only serves veteran-owned businesses but there are veterans groups on the investing side of the platform too. What this means, and this is no small thing, is that veterans believe they are borrowing from their fellow veterans (and not just borrowing from you). That equates to some of the lowest default rates in the industry. Streetshares also has a non-profit foundation that serves veterans' groups.

Minimum Investment: $25
Rates: 5% fixed
Term: Very short term, maximum 36 month loans
Liquidity: Funds are locked up for 12 months and available after that time.
IRA Accepted?: Yes, they work with Millennium Trust as custodian if you don't have a custodian that allows this and you need a self directed IRA
Types of Property: Business assets, Accounts Receivable/Inventory, Equipment
Safety: Likely have little to no collateral. Your protection is the idea of veterans borrowing from veterans. Truly, it is.
More Info: Their Veteran Business Bonds landing page at www.streetshares.com

Summary
There's a lot of meat in this chapter. That's thanks to Reg A+. This amendment makes capital raising in general, and peer to peer lending platforms in specific more accessible to more people.

Five different online marketplace lending platforms have opted for this method of making their platform available to retail investors. Four of them: RealtyMogul, Fundrise, GroundFloor, and AHP all present unique characteristics and different investment options for real estate investors. Whether it is a REIT-style investment with RM and Fundrise, rehab based investments with Ground Floor, or delinquent mortgage buying with AHP, all present options that can make money over a long term period of time from a reputable platform in the industry. The fifth, Streetshares, is a small business lending platform that focuses on veterans and, like the REIT-style investments (without the property), investment on Streetshares are spread across their entire platform of available loans.

Here's that table I promised:

Summary of Reg A+ Peer to Peer Lending Platforms

	RealtyMogul	Fundrise	GroundFloor	AHP	Streetshares
Type of Platform	Real Estate	Real Estate	Real Estate	Real Estate	Small Business
Min Investment	1000	1000	10	100	25
Rate Sought	10%+	10%+	10%+	12%	5%
Rate Fixed?	N	N	N	Y	Y
Rate Guaranteed?	N	N	N	N	N
Term	Long Term	Long Term	Short Term	Long Term	1 year
Liquidity	Y	Y, but limited	Y	Y	Y, after 1 year
IRAs Accepted?	Y	Y	Y	Y	Y
Types of Collateral	Comm Property	Comm Property	Residential Property	Residential Property	Business Assets or None
Safety	Secured by Prop	Secured by Prop	Secured by Prop	Secured by Prop	Secured by Biz Assets
More Info	realtymogul.com	fundrise.com	groundfloor.us	ahpfund.com	streetshares.com

With 5 choices, you are likely to find something that fits your level of risk and comfort and all of them make it very easy on their websites to set up and fund an account. Do your own due diligence on a platform before you invest.

Lastly, I think it important to list my personal disclosures. At the time of this writing, I have no investments on any of these platforms (although I expect that to change soon with at least one of the platforms mentioned in this chapter). I do have a business relationship with one of them, where I do some writing for them. That writing is online content for their website and is not in any way meant to steer you to one of the platforms over any of the others.

Chapter 7: The Stalwarts: Lending Club & Prosper

After the 5 platforms covered in the last chapter, you may feel some p2p lending exhaustion. I understand. We are only going to cover 2 more in this chapter. They are the two most important, longest operating platforms and the most visible to the public. They are Lending Club and Prosper. They deserve a chapter to themselves.

Other commonalities include they both do consumer unsecured lending as their primary form of lending. This means that individual consumers are borrowing, most often to consolidate existing credit cards into a lower rate loan up to $35,000. They both went with the most expensive and compliance required method to open to retail investors by doing S-1 filings with the SEC. They both have loans outstanding in the billions of dollars. Both were the guinea pigs to establish the proof of concept for p2p lending in the US in the first place.

Also in common, I invest my own personal funds on both of these platforms.

As you can see, they have quite a bit in common. They do have some differences, too. Time to dig in a little deeper.

Lending Club

Out of the 7 platforms open to retail investors, Lending Club is the only one that is a publicly traded company. It trades on the NYSE under the symbol LC and currently trades at just under $5 per share.

I'm no investment adviser so I'm not advising you on whether you should buy the stock or not. I'm here to show you why you should be lending on the Lending Club platform.

Lending Club started back in 2007 when it issued its first loan. Here's a brief look at its history.

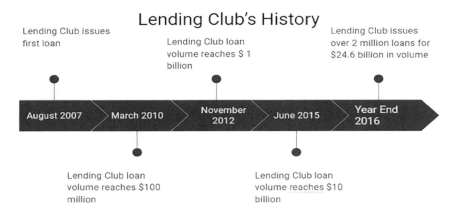

In 9 years, they've done over 2 million loans for a total of $24.6 billion in loan volume so you don't have to worry about being first to lend there or with LC having to 'work out the kinks' because their process is new. And there's lots of room to grow as Lending Club's own About Us page indicates that the consumer lending market is a $3 trillion market[41]. LC Board member John Mack used to run investment bank Morgan Stanley and is their Chairman Emeritus. He says that Lending Club 'has created an innovative platform that provides investors with low cost access to high quality consumer credit assets, and at the same time makes credit more affordable to consumers'[42]. BlackRock is one of the institutional investors, funds and other smart money investing on Lending Club[43]. BlackRock invests on Prosper as well.[44]

LC is among the most transparent of all the platforms as they have their own Statistics Page where you can look at and download all the loan data. I'm a big fan of this kind of openness.

---

[41] https://www.lendingclub.com/public/about-us.action See Our Growth
[42] https://www.lendingclub.com/public/about-us.action See Our Awards
[43] https://www.bloomberg.com/news/articles/2015-02-02/blackrock-finds-few-peers-with-330-million-book-of-online-loans
[44] https://www.bloomberg.com/news/articles/2015-02-02/blackrock-finds-few-peers-with-330-million-book-of-online-loans

Lending Club allows IRA investment on their platform. How much you earn and how much risk you take is entirely up to you. In the next chapter we cover 2 popular investing strategies. They have 7 loan grades from A-G. Here are the current rates that they pay to us and charge to the borrowers:

Loan Grade	Interest Rate	Origination Fee	36-Month APR	60-Month APR
A	5.32% - 7.99%	1% - 5%*	5.99% - 11.51%	7.46% - 10.19%
B	8.24% - 11.49%	5%	11.77% - 15.08%	10.44% - 13.76%
C	12.74% - 15.99%	6%	17.12% - 20.46%	15.52% - 18.86%
D	16.99% - 21.49%	6%	21.48% - 26.11%	19.89% - 24.53%
E	19.99% - 26.24%	6%	24.57% - 31.00%	22.98% - 29.43%
F	24.24% - 30.74%	6%	28.94% - 35.63%	27.36% - 34.08%
G	28.55% - 30.99%	6%	33.37% - 35.89%	31.82% - 34.34%

Note that the rates have ranges. This is because each grade has 3 sub-grades so in the A loan grade, you have A1, A2, and A3, each of which pays a different rate and A3 is a lower rate than B1 and it goes down the line to G3.

Terms are 3 years or 5 years for the borrowers and they can pay off at anytime with no prepayment penalty, and that does happen from time to time. The origination fee listed here is for the BORROWERS, not for you as an investor. However, you do have to pay a 1% servicing fee each month based on what Lending Club collects to service the loan, process the payments and pay you what you are owed. It's a small price to pay to help keep your investments organized.

Great Filtering and Investing Options

Lending Club has an autoinvest feature so you can set your parameters and it will just keep investing for you. Many investors use this feature and love it. I do not use it myself. I like manual selection. With a minimum investment of $25 per loan it is easy to spread your risk out over many borrowers.

This is what the Loan Selection page looks like:

Manual Investing

Invite Friends

« back
Available: Sign In

Showing Loans 1 - 15 of 465

Add to Order

<< < 1 2 3 4 5 > >> 15 ▼

	Rate	Term	FICO®	Amount	Purpose	% Funded	Amount / Time Left
Build a Portfolio	E 2	60	670-674	$16,575	Credit Card Payoff	99%	$25 / 22 days
Per Loan: $25	23.99%						
	D 3	60	675-679	$30,000	Loan Refinancing & Consolidation	97%	$900 / 21 days
Filter Loans	18.99%						
Loan Term ▼	C 1	60	670-674	$32,000	Other	88%	$3,625 / 28 days
☑ 36-month	12.74%						
☑ 60-month	E 2	60	680-684	$35,000	Credit Card Payoff	84%	$5,425 / 22 days
	23.99%						
Interest Rate ▼	C 5	36	665-669	$4,800	Loan Refinancing & Consolidation	92%	$350 / 28 days
☑ All ☐ 17.47%	15.99%						
☐ A 6.80% ☐ 21.36%	D 4	36	670-674	$5,000	Home Improvement	86%	$700 / 28 days
☐ B 9.93% ☐ F 25.77%	19.99%						
☐ C 13.38% ☐ G 28.83%	D 4	36	670-674	$4,000	Credit Card Payoff	88%	$450 / 29 days
	19.99%						
Keyword▶	B 2	36	680-684	$3,000	Loan Refinancing & Consolidation	80%	$575 / 29 days
Exclude Loans already invested in▶	10.49%						
	E	60	695-699	$30,000	Loan Refinancing & Consolidation	89%	$3,100 / 24 days
More Filters »	26.24%						
Update Results	D 2	36	690-694	$12,200	Loan Refinancing & Consolidation	85%	$1,775 / 27 days
	17.99%						
Minimize All Reset All	B 2	36	660-664	$6,800	Credit Card Payoff	88%	$750 / 28 days
	10.49%						

Down the entire left side you can choose up to 40 data points to filter loans from FICO credit score to LC loan grade to loan term like only 36 month loans to whether the borrower owns a home or not.

When you open your account you should play around with the filters and see what kind of results you get. You can also start small and mix and match. My colleague Anil Gupta at his great site PeerCube allows for backtesting of Lending Club and Prosper loan data with the filters you have selected to see how effective they were, and all for free. What happened in the past does not mean it will happen in the future, but there's still great testing information if you have your own ideas about what you want to invest in.

Risks

Most of Lending Club's risks are the same risk as all peer to peer lending platforms. We covered the big 3 risks of full economic cycle risk, liquidity risk and platform risk in Chapter 4. A platform specific risk to Lending Club is credit risk.

Credit risk: Will the borrowers pay? Unlike the real estate platforms where you have security with the property, these loans are entirely unsecured. You and I both know that if a borrower is struggling they are likely to let their LC loan go unpaid instead of their mortgage. Understanding this is vital to understanding the risk in marketplace loans generally and in LC specifically.

Lending Club also has some management based risk. Last spring they had to oust their founder over some loans that they sold to an institutional investor that did not meet that investor's criteria[45]. The founder did this knowingly to sell the loans so he was ousted along with some other senior executives. The COO Scott Sanborn was named CEO and has been in the position for a year now. He seems to have righted the ship. Institutional investors, including the one involved in the fraudulent sale, are back on the platform[46].

Summary

Minimum investment: $25, no minimum to open account
Rates: Variable based on loan grade from 5% up to 30%
Term: Loans are 3 years or 5 years
Liquidity: Cash balance available anytime. Investment in active loans not liquid with no secondary market
IRA accepted?: Yes through partnership with IRA custodian Self Directed IRA Services..
Types of Collateral: None

---

[45] http://www.cnbc.com/2016/05/09/lending-club-shares-tumble-after-ceo-resigns.html
[46] http://www.businessinsider.com/lending-club-is-on-a-path-to-recovery-2016-11

Safety: These are prime borrowers, the best personal credits in the country and they usually care about keeping good credit. There is NO collateral backing the loan.
More Info: LendingClub.com

Prosper

Prosper is also a consumer, unsecured lender. I made my own first p2p investment with Prosper and still find it the most user-friendly platform. Prosper is the oldest lending platform started in 2006, but it took till 2009 to really start getting some traction as an investment platform.

Prosper's loan grades differ from Lending Club as they have an HR rate (for high rate) and a AA rate. The AA is the highest grade, followed by A-E and then HR. Prosper has its own proprietary score from 1-11 where higher is better. Per their prospectus, the score is a measure of the likelihood of a default on the loan[47]. Prosper has an AutoInvest feature as well and a $25 per loan minimum.

Prosper's last rate increase was in late 2016 and here are the current rates[48]

$ Weighted Borrower Rate			
Prosper Rating	September 2016	Simulation	Difference (Simulated - Sep 2016)
AA	6.75%	6.33%	-0.42%
A	9.21%	8.51%	-0.70%
B	12.20%	11.50%	-0.70%
C	17.15%	16.36%	-0.79%
D	23.01%	23.20%	0.19%
E	28.27%	29.01%	0.74%
HR	31.38%	31.92%	0.54%
Total	14.47%	14.08%	-0.39%

---

[47] https://www.prosper.com/Downloads/Legal/Prosper_Prospectus_2017-04-07.pdf p.46-47
[48] https://www.prosper.com/about-us/2016/10/25/prosper-announces-pricing-change/?bid=74&bname=Investor%20Updates

The rates are comparable to Lending Club although the change in rates is a slight drop across the board.

Here is what Prosper's loan selection page looks like:

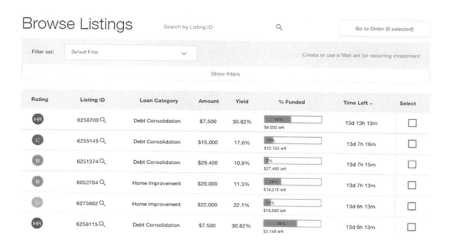

Their filters are up at the top in purple saying Show Filters. They also have many filters you can choose and you can use PeerCube to backtest them.

The smart money is also investing on Prosper including a recent $5 billion deal with the Soros Investment fund and Investment Bank Jefferies LLC[49]. This deal was in February of this year and is the biggest loan purchase deal in the history of the industry. Again, this helps to show that it's not too late to get started if you haven't invested in marketplace loans until now.

Risks

Prosper and Lending Club share many of the same risks including our big 3 that all platforms share and credit risk, which is a bigger factor

---

[49] https://www.wsj.com/articles/prosper-inks-5-billion-loan-buying-dealwith-investors-including-soros-jefferies-1488222470

for Lending Club and Prosper than for other platforms since the loans have no collateral.

Prosper has a new CEO[50], David Kimball, who was the CFO and before that had been at another very service oriented financial company, the military centric USAA. The previous CEO, Aaron Vermut, did a great job managing through difficult circumstances like navigating the SEC regulatory environment. Kimball will be expected to scale up the business to get to a scale that more closely resembles Lending Club. One of his first actions since taking over in late November was negotiating the $5 billion deal that just closed in February. Their President Emeritus, Ron Suber, is one of the lions of the industry and Ron still advises Prosper in his Emeritus status.

The new management is so far, so good, but new management is always a question mark. Almost one year in, the management is doing well.

Minimum investment: $25
Rates: Variable based on loan grade from 5% to 30+%
Term: Loans are 3 years or 5 years
Liquidity: Cash balance available immediately. Funds in active loans illiquid and no secondary market available.
IRA accepted?: Yes, they work with Millennium Trust Company
Types of Collateral: None
Safety: The best credits, like at LC, who want to preserve their credit. Loan is unsecured. No collateral
More Info: Prosper.com

Summary
Lending Club and Prosper are the kings of online marketplace lending, especially when it comes to where retail investors can invest their money. They are the largest and longest running platforms. Both

---

[50] https://www.prosper.com/about-us/2016/11/14/prosper-marketplace-names-david-kimball-chief-executive-officer/

are consumer unsecured lending so the risks of full economic cycle risk, liquidity risk and platform risk still apply. We have the additional credit risk with both since the loans have no collateral. Despite the lack of collateral, we have a better balance of risk vs return for how we invest our money and the loan grades are so widely varying that you can invest in very conservative to very high yield seeking loans or mix and match to your liking.

The purpose of going over these risks is not to show that marketplace loans are riskless compared to bonds or other fixed income investments. We want to show that the risks here are much more open and transparent than the risks associated with bonds PLUS we are compensated for the risks we take whether we invest in A or AA loans or E and HR loans.

Chapter 8: The P2P Investment Strategy

After talking about the 5 Reg A+ peer to peer lending platforms AND Lending Club and Prosper, you've seen that you have 7 investment options as a retail investor in 2017.

If you believe like I do, that p2p lending is a better fixed income investment option for that portion of your overall portfolio instead of bonds, then the next natural question is "How do I invest?" or what is the best strategy?

Bond mutual funds became popular for investment since you buy a piece of many bonds and it allows for small regular investments instead of having to buy a bond at par ($1000) each time you want to buy. Having to wait until you have $1000 to buy a single bond is not efficient investing. Bond mutual funds are more user friendly than buying individual bonds. Peer lending platforms are user friendly in this way too.

Before we go over the strategy, let's compare all 7 platforms against each other. This table is a copy of the Reg A+ table in Chapter 6 with Lending Club and Prosper added.

Platform	RealtyMogul	Fundrise	GroundFloor	AHP
Type of Platform	Real Estate	Real Estate	Real Estate	Real Estate
Min Investment	1000	1000	10	100
Rate Sought	10%+	10%+	10%+	12%
Rate Fixed?	N	N	N	Y
Rate Guaranteed?	N	N	N	N
Term	Long Term	Long Term	Short Term	Long Term
Liquidity	Y	Y, but limited	Y	Y
IRAs Accepted?	Y	Y	Y	Y
Types of Collateral	Comm Property (Apartments)	Comm Property	Residential Property	Residential Property
Safety	Secured by Prop	Secured by Prop	Secured by Prop	Secured by Prop
More Info	realtymogul.com	fundrise.com	groundfloor.us	ahpfund.com

Platform	Streetshares	Lending Club	Prosper	
Type of Platform	Small Business	Consumer	Consumer	
Min Investment	25	25	25	
Rate Sought	5%	Varies by loan grade	Varies by loan grade	
Rate Fixed?	Y	N	N	
Rate Guaranteed?	N	N	N	
Term	1 year	3 or 5 years	3 or 5 years	
Liquidity	Y, after 1 year	Y, partial	Y, partial	
IRAs Accepted?	Y	Y	Y	
Types of Collateral	Business Assets or None	None	None	
Safety	Secured by Biz Assets	Unsecured Loan	Unsecured Loan	
More Info	streetshares.com	lendingclub.com	prosper.com	

Thanks to the generally low minimum investment amounts, it helps to outline the most effective strategy.

Monthly Investment Strategy

Due to 401k or IRA investments and stock or bond mutual funds, we are conditioned to investing in small periodic investments over time. Those periods are usually either monthly or every 2 weeks for those that invest through a payroll deduction.

To substitute p2p lending for what would be some or all of your bond investment, there's no reason to fight this tendency. Use it to your advantage. Since 5 of the 7 platforms have a minimum investment of $100 or less, you should be investing monthly into new loans.

The investor login side at all the platforms is full of good information, tracking of your investments and cash balance and other data about your investments that are very useful and user-friendly. Many also have autoinvest features so you can set it and it keeps investing for you.

Here are 2 common ways to use monthly investing to earn Interest through peer to peer lending.

Two Common Investment Strategies: Proxy Savings and The Yield Seeker

Strategy 1: The Proxy Savings

One of the most common investing strategies is what I call the Proxy Savings Account. Savings accounts at banks used to pay interest high enough that it was more than inflation and would encourage us to save. However, this has not been true of banking for some time.

With a p2p investing strategy, we can replicate the savings account of old. Using Lending Club and Prosper as an example, investing at least 80% of our p2p lending money into A grade Lending Club loans and AA and A grade Prosper loans means you have the potential to earn 4.5%-6.5% depending on loan grades and losses.

The benefits of this strategy are that you are investing in the very best credits these platforms offer. Doing this and investing in many loans reduces credit risk significantly, which was one of the big risks of lending on LC or Prosper. The downside is the limitation in the potential returns you can earn by concentrating on the A and AA credits. However, you can still invest some funds in one of the other platforms.

For instance, this is a way to mirror the Proxy Savings Account while trying to earn some additional returns with $5000: (note the platforms selected are NOT direct recommendations over the 3 I didn't choose)

Platform	Amount Invested	Credit Grade	Potential Returns	Interest Earned 1 Year
Lending Club (40%)	2000	A	5.32-7.99%	106.40 (at 5.32%)
Prosper (40%)	2000	AA and A	6.7-9.2%	134 (at 6.7%)
AHP (10%)	500	Across all grades	12%	60
Streetshares (10%)	500	Across all grades	5%	25
Total	5000		**6.50%**	325.40

With 80% in LC and Prosper, the foundation of the returns are in the A and AA loans and even in these high credit grades, there will be some losses. Hopefully, they will be insignificant. At the lowest returns on LC and Prosper (5.32% and 6.7%), this portfolio can return 6.5% annually. This is a pretty nice return for a conservative strategy.

Strategy 2: The Yield Seeker

On the other end of the risk/return spectrum is the Yield Seeker. The yield seeker decides to invest in high rate loans, taking the losses as they come, and hoping to make a better than average yield once it's all said and done.

With this strategy, 80% of our money invests on Lending Club and Prosper again. This time F and G rated loans on LC and E and HR loans on Prosper. Loss rates on Prosper are between 15-20% at these grades[51]. Lending Club's loss rates are 21% across all F and G loans and 15% on E grade loans across their history[52].

In early November 2017, LC made a change in loan offerings following their 3rd Quarter 2017 earnings announcement. F and G rated loans are **NO LONGER OFFERED** on the platform[53]. E is the lowest grade remaining on Lending Club.

---

[51] https://www.prosper.com/Downloads/Legal/Prosper_Prospectus_2017-04-28.pdf P. 54-58
[52] https://www.lendingclub.com/info/demand-and-credit-profile.action Loan Performance Update chart
[53] https://help.lendingclub.com/hc/en-us/articles/115014049387-Changes-to-Grade-Offerings-on-the-LendingClub-Platform Investor Updates

With the remaining 20% invested elsewhere, a yield seeking portfolio might look like this with $5000.

Platform	Amount Invested	Credit Grade	Potential Returns	Expected Losses	Interest Earned
Lending Club (40%)	2000	E	20-26%	15.24%	96 (at 20%)
Prosper (40%)	2000	E and HR	28-32%	15-20%	340 (at 32%)
AHP (20%)	1000	Across all grades	12%	minimal	120
Total	5000		**11.12%**		556

By understanding the risks you are willing to take, even with defaults, you can still get a double digit return and a return that doubles the much more conservative Proxy Savings account strategy. Does that mean you should do this strategy? Not necessarily. The defaults that WILL come are not for the faint of heart. Good loan selection is critical to try to lower the credit risk.

These 2 strategies are not recommendations. I don't do investment advice for a living. These are just for illustrative purposes of 2 ways that people invest in p2p loans as a substitute for bonds.

There are no quality bond returns approaching the Proxy Savings 6.5% return let alone the Yield Seeking returns. The risk you must take in bonds to get 6.5% seems far greater than investing in the very best credits on a marketplace lending platform. Our high yield 'junk bond' rate from Chapter 3 was 6.44% in the NYT. This much more conservative strategy pays 6 basis points more (0.06%) and risk is much, much less.

I don't do either of these strategies. I mix and match to try to find mispriced loans, loans where I think they are a B credit but are priced as a C credit as an example. If you want to learn more about how I do that then check out the Lending Club and Prosper tags for articles on my blog at P2PLendingExpert.com.

One last topic to address when it comes to investments: Taxes.

Taxes

I'm no tax professional. Please talk to yours. That's my disclaimer....

Now that that's out of the way, I will tell you my experience with taxes on peer to peer lending as an investment. We generally have 2 things to account for: Interest and Defaulted loans.
When it comes to Interest, the platform will send you the 1099-INT that everyone else sends you when you earn Interest on an investment. Banks and brokerages send this form every year. That Interest is taxable and goes on the Schedule B of your 1040, which covers interest and dividends. If you are in a tax-deferred investment like an IRA, then you don't have to worry about this. Your Interest goes in Part 1 of the form

SCHEDULE B (Form 1040A or 1040) (Rev. January 2017) Department of the Treasury Internal Revenue Service (99)	Interest and Ordinary Dividends ► Attach to Form 1040A or 1040. ► Information about Schedule B and its instructions is at www.irs.gov/scheduleb.	OMB No. 1545-0074 2016 Attachment Sequence No. 08
Name(s) shown on return		Your social security number

Part I Interest	1	List name of payer. If any interest is from a seller-financed mortgage and the buyer used the property as a personal residence, see instructions on back and list this interest first. Also, show that buyer's social security number and address ►		Amount
(See instructions on back and the instructions for Form 1040A, or Form 1040, line 8a.)			1	
Note: If you received a Form 1099-INT, Form 1099-OID, or substitute statement from a brokerage firm, list the firm's name as the payer and enter the total interest shown on that form.	2	Add the amounts on line 1	2	
	3	Excludable interest on series EE and I U.S. savings bonds issued after 1989. Attach Form 8815	3	
	4	Subtract line 3 from line 2. Enter the result here and on Form 1040A, or Form 1040, line 8a . . . . ►	4	
		Note: If line 4 is over $1,500, you must complete Part III.		Amount

Your total interest (line 4) goes right to your 1040 form meaning you pay your ordinary income tax rate (your marginal tax rate). So if your tax rate is 28%, then you will be paying that 28% on this and all your other interest earned.

Defaulted loans are a little more complicated. I have seen numerous advisors say that when a loan defaults that we must declare a capital loss on the principal we won't be getting. The most common form to use for a Gain on Sale of an Asset (or in our case Loss on Sale) is the form 4797. Here it is.

Form **4797**	**Sales of Business Property** (Also Involuntary Conversions and Recapture Amounts Under Sections 179 and 280F(b)(2))	OMB No. 1545-0184 **20**16
Department of the Treasury Internal Revenue Service	► Attach to your tax return. ► Information about Form 4797 and its separate instructions is at *www.irs.gov/form4797*.	Attachment Sequence No. **27**
Name(s) shown on return		Identifying number

1 Enter the gross proceeds from sales or exchanges reported to you for 2016 on Form(s) 1099-B or 1099-S (or substitute statement) that you are including on line 2, 10, or 20. See instructions 1

Part I Sales or Exchanges of Property Used in a Trade or Business and Involuntary Conversions From Other Than Casualty or Theft—Most Property Held More Than 1 Year (see instructions)

2	(a) Description of property	(b) Date acquired (mo., day, yr.)	(c) Date sold (mo., day, yr.)	(d) Gross sales price	(e) Depreciation allowed or allowable since acquisition	(f) Cost or other basis, plus improvements and expense of sale	(g) Gain or (loss) Subtract (f) from the sum of (d) and (e)

3 Gain, if any, from Form 4684, line 39 3
4 Section 1231 gain from installment sales from Form 6252, line 26 or 37 4
5 Section 1231 gain or (loss) from like-kind exchanges from Form 8824 5
6 Gain, if any, from line 32, from other than casualty or theft 6
7 Combine lines 2 through 6. Enter the gain or (loss) here and on the appropriate line as follows: 7

Partnerships (except electing large partnerships) and S corporations. Report the gain or (loss) following the instructions for Form 1065, Schedule K, line 10, or Form 1120S, Schedule K, line 9. Skip lines 8, 9, 11, and 12 below.

Individuals, partners, S corporation shareholders, and all others. If line 7 is zero or a loss, enter the amount from line 7 on line 11 below and skip lines 8 and 9. If line 7 is a gain and you didn't have any prior year section 1231 losses, or they were recaptured in an earlier year, enter the gain from line 7 as a long-term capital gain on the Schedule D filed with your return and skip lines 8, 9, 11, and 12 below.

8 Nonrecaptured net section 1231 losses from prior years. See instructions 8
9 Subtract line 8 from line 7. If zero or less, enter -0-. If line 9 is zero, enter the gain from line 7 on line 12 below. If line 9 is more than zero, enter the amount from line 8 on line 12 below and enter the gain from line 9 as a long-term capital gain on the Schedule D filed with your return. See instructions 9

Part II Ordinary Gains and Losses (see instructions)

10 Ordinary gains and losses not included on lines 11 through 16 (include property held 1 year or less):

Losses you claim here may go against other income depending on how long you had the loan before it went to default and other factors. Again, please consult your tax professional as I am not one.

Summary on Taxes
Not only will you have less annual tracking of taxable income, but your custodian will be handling it instead of you or your CPA if you use a

tax deferred investment like an IRA or solo 401k to hold your p2p loans for investment purposes.

If you invest through an open, taxable account, then you have an annual responsibility to track Interest earned as well as your losses from Default so you can claim those gains and losses on your annual personal tax return each year.

Conclusion

Retail investors have 7 marketplace lending platform choices to choose from where you can decide how much risk you want to take on your fixed income investments. I've made the argument that anywhere from some to all your portfolio allocation you would make for bonds should go to this new asset class. You get to exert much more control over how much risk you want to take and the returns you may generate as a result of those risks. This risks are more transparent unlike what GM bondholders went through. In this chapter, we have the handy chart comparing all 7 on many features. We also looked at why you should invest monthly just like you would in a mutual fund. I explained two common investment strategies, the Proxy Savings and the Yield Seeker, in more detail to show different ways to invest in p2p loans and how to select the risks you want to take.

I hope if you have any comments about this book or your investment experiences in peer to peer loans that you will come to my blog at P2PLendingExpert.com and join the conversation. If you are interested in learning more about this subject, you can subscribe for free and get tips and techniques in your mailbox once a month.

Good luck and successful investing.

About The Author

Stu Lustman is the blogmaster at P2PLendingExpert.com, which he started in 2013. Stu has worked his entire career in finance before getting into financial writing and now writes full time for online p2p lenders, conventional finance companies, Bitcoin/blockchain companies, equipment leasing companies, and service providers to the financial industry. He's a sought after speaker in the online lending, Bitcoin, and equipment leasing industries and speaks at a couple conferences per year.

Stu is originally from Baltimore, Maryland and lives in Atlanta. He has a BA from the University of Maryland and an MBA from Loyola University. Other than finance, his interests include coffee, cooking, homebrewing, traveling, and trying to improve his terrible Spanish.

Printed in Great Britain
by Amazon

30061160R00041